# I WOULDN'T LET ...
# A CAT TEACH ME TO SKYDIVE

By Paul Mason and Pipi Sposito

WAYLAND

First published in Great Britain in 2026
by Wayland
© Hodder and Stoughton, 2026
All rights reserved

Credits:
Series Editor: Melanie Palmer
Design: Lisa Peacock
Illustrations: Pipi Sposito

ISBN HB 978 1 5263 3094 9
ISBN PB 978 1 5263 3095 6

Printed and bound in Dubai

Wayland
An imprint of
Hachette Children's Group
Part of Hodder and Stoughton
Carmelite House
50 Victoria Embankment
London EC4Y 0DZ

An Hachette UK Company
www.hachette.co.uk
www.hachettechildrens.co.uk

The authorised representative in the EEA is Hachette Ireland, 8 Castlecourt Centre, Dublin 15, D15 XTP3, Ireland (email: info@hbgi.ie).

MIX
Paper | Supporting responsible forestry
FSC® C104740

# CONTENTS

| | |
|---|---|
| A kitten's dream | 4 |
| You can't avoid gravity | 6 |
| Skydiving school for cats | 8 |
| How parachutes work | 10 |
| Parachute-packing class | 12 |
| Ripping force | 14 |
| Time for takeoff | 16 |
| How a plane takes off | 18 |
| A secret mission | 20 |
| The route to Mousetown | 22 |
| Skydiving cats | 24 |
| Cats CAN swim | 26 |
| Safely ashore | 28 |
| Bonus cat facts | 30 |
| Glossary | 31 |
| Index | 32 |

# YOU CAN'T AVOID GRAVITY

The kitten fell off the wall because of a force called gravity.

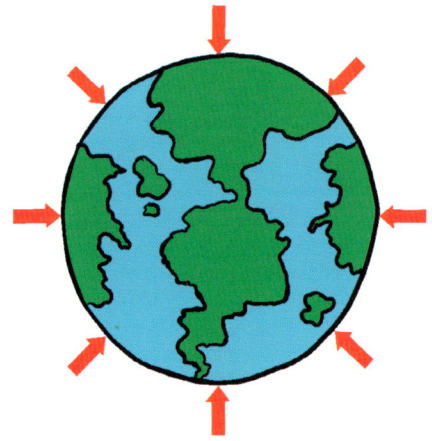

Gravity is a pulling force. It pulls all of us toward the Earth.

**WHAT WOULD WE DO WITHOUT GRAVITY?**

"We'd float off into space!"

"Help!"

"Not sure I like this."

So gravity is a good thing.

# SKYDIVING SCHOOL FOR CATS

The kitten eventually grew up. But it never forgot its dream of defeating gravity – or at least, slowing it down.

# HOW PARACHUTES WORK

What makes a skydiver fall so slowly? It's a force called air resistance.

Air resistance is a kind of friction. Friction is a pulling force between two things, if one or both of the things is moving.

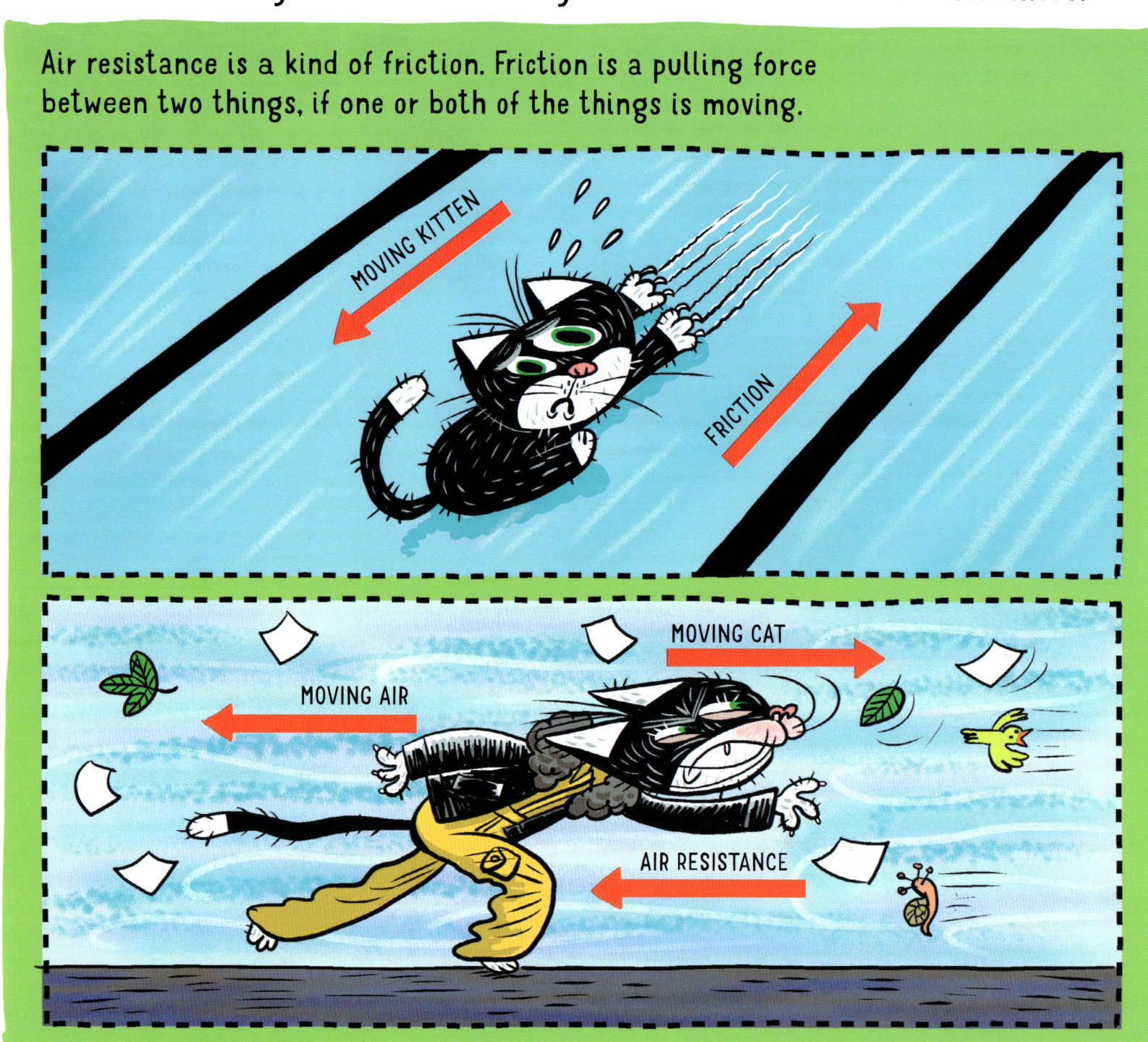

Big shapes feel more air resistance than small ones:

Parachutes are always much bigger than what's dangling from them. The extra air resistance slows down the object's fall.

# RIPPING FORCE

To know the parachute would rip, the cat needed to understand weight and materials.

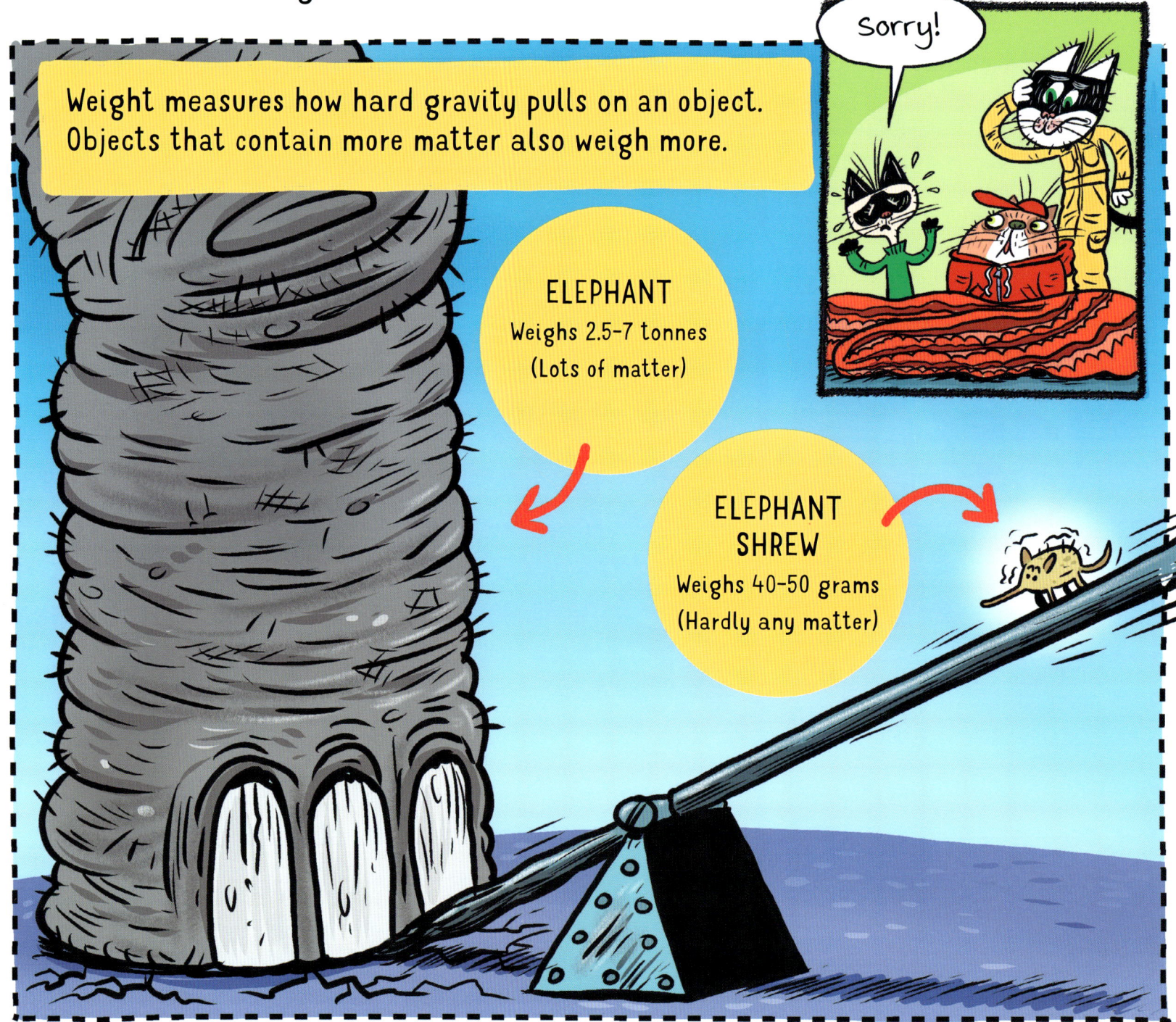

Weight measures how hard gravity pulls on an object. Objects that contain more matter also weigh more.

ELEPHANT
Weighs 2.5-7 tonnes
(Lots of matter)

ELEPHANT SHREW
Weighs 40-50 grams
(Hardly any matter)

Sorry!

# HOW A PLANE TAKES OFF

The cats didn't like it when their plane took off. It felt like an impossible thing was happening.

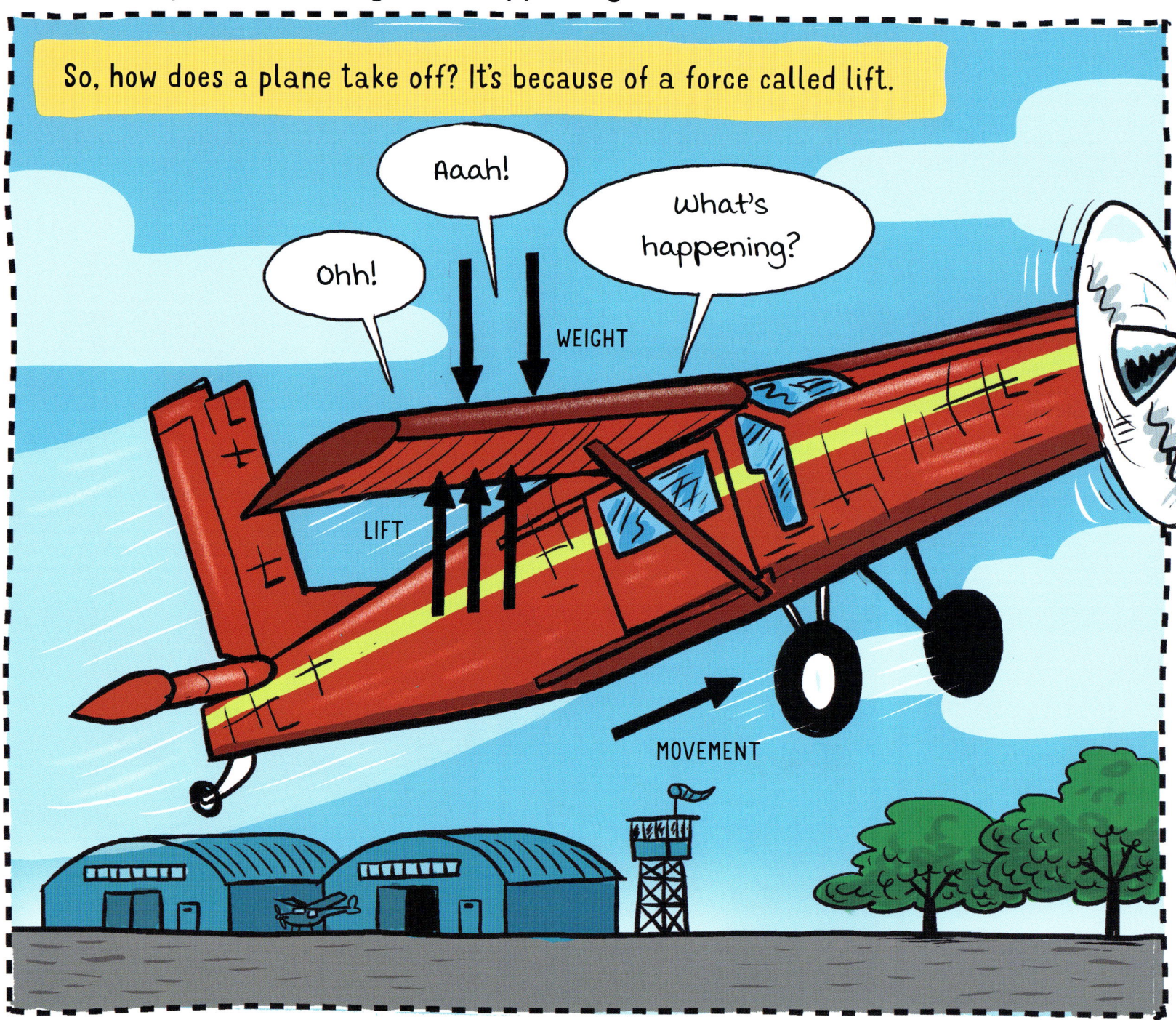

# A SECRET MISSION

The best place to land from a parachute jump is a wide area of flat land.

# THE ROUTE TO MOUSETOWN

How will the pilot find the way to Mousetown?
The force we call magnetism will help.

Magnetism is a pulling force. It works on a few metals, such as iron.

Magnet

Iron nails

Earth is magnetic, so the iron arrow in a compass points north-south.

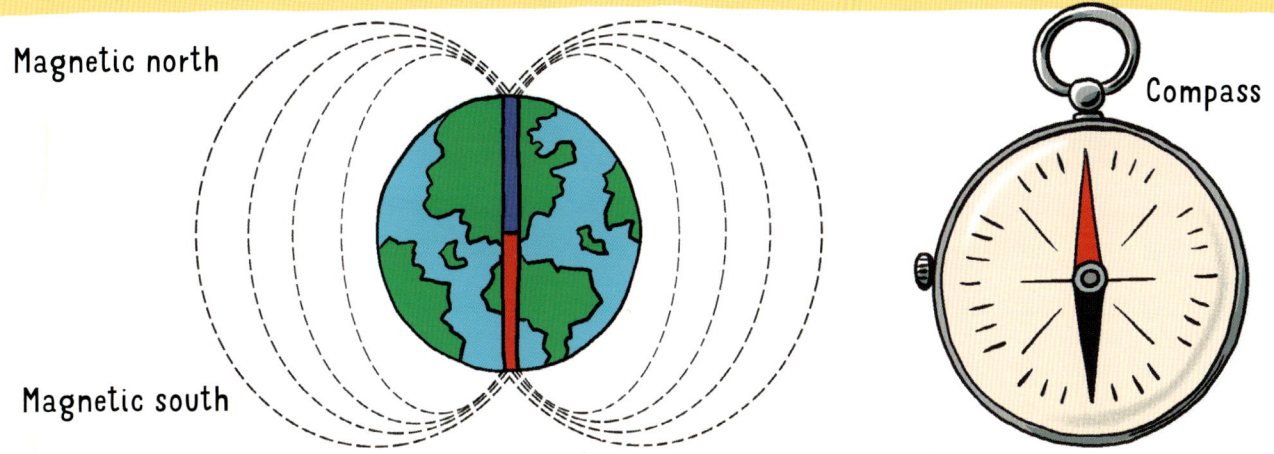

The pilot's map shows that Mousetown is north of where they are now.

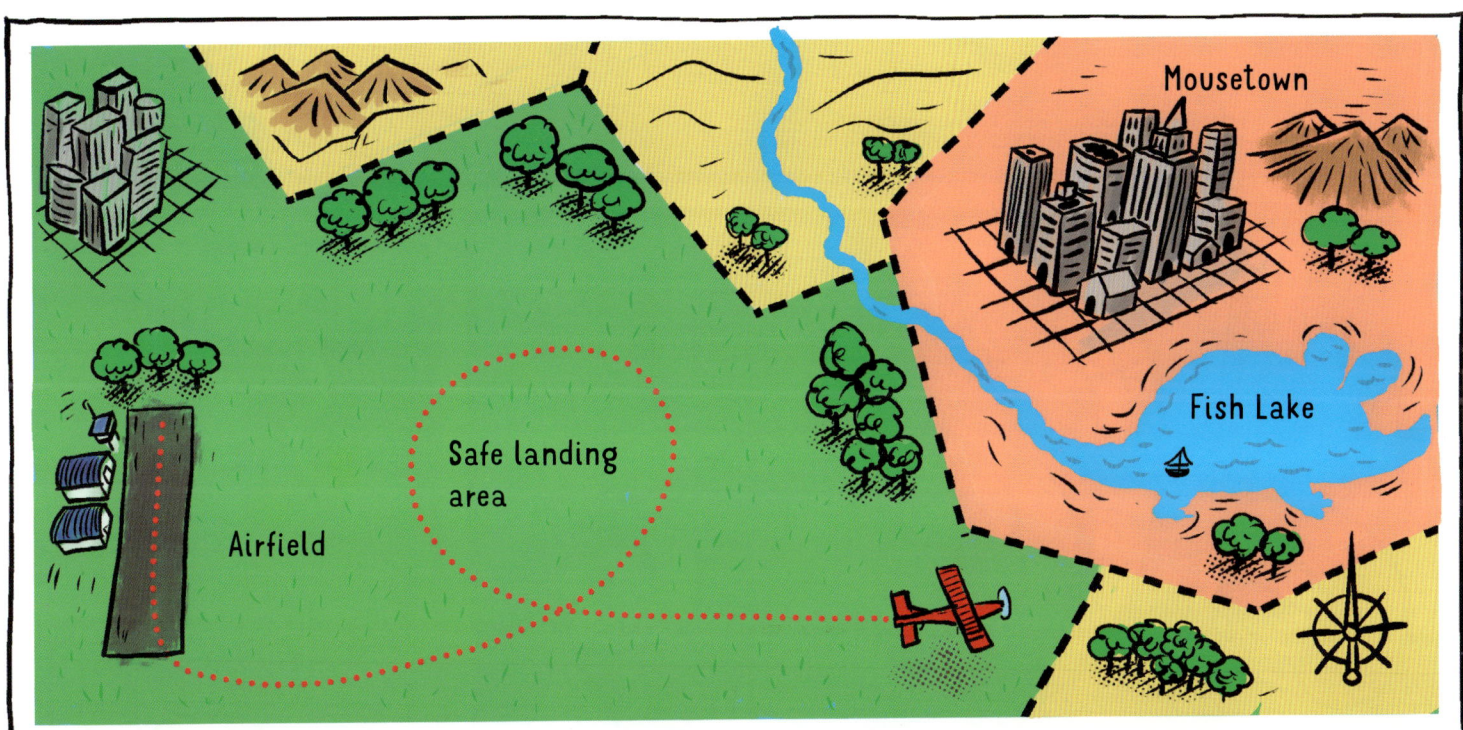

The planeload of skydiving cats sets off for Mousetown.

# SKYDIVING CATS

It's the moment of truth for the skydiving cats. Their plane has arrived at Mousetown.

BRRRRRRRRRRRR

"mousetown, here we come!"

The cats haven't counted on the wind starting to blow ...

"Hang on ..."

"We're being blown off course."

... and they get a landing they weren't expecting.

SPLASH

"Oh no!"

"I hate swimming."

"I see a fish! Yum!"

# CATS CAN SWIM

They just really don't like it ...

A kind of friction called water resistance pulled against the cats' bodies. The fish escaped because its streamlined shape created less water resistance*.

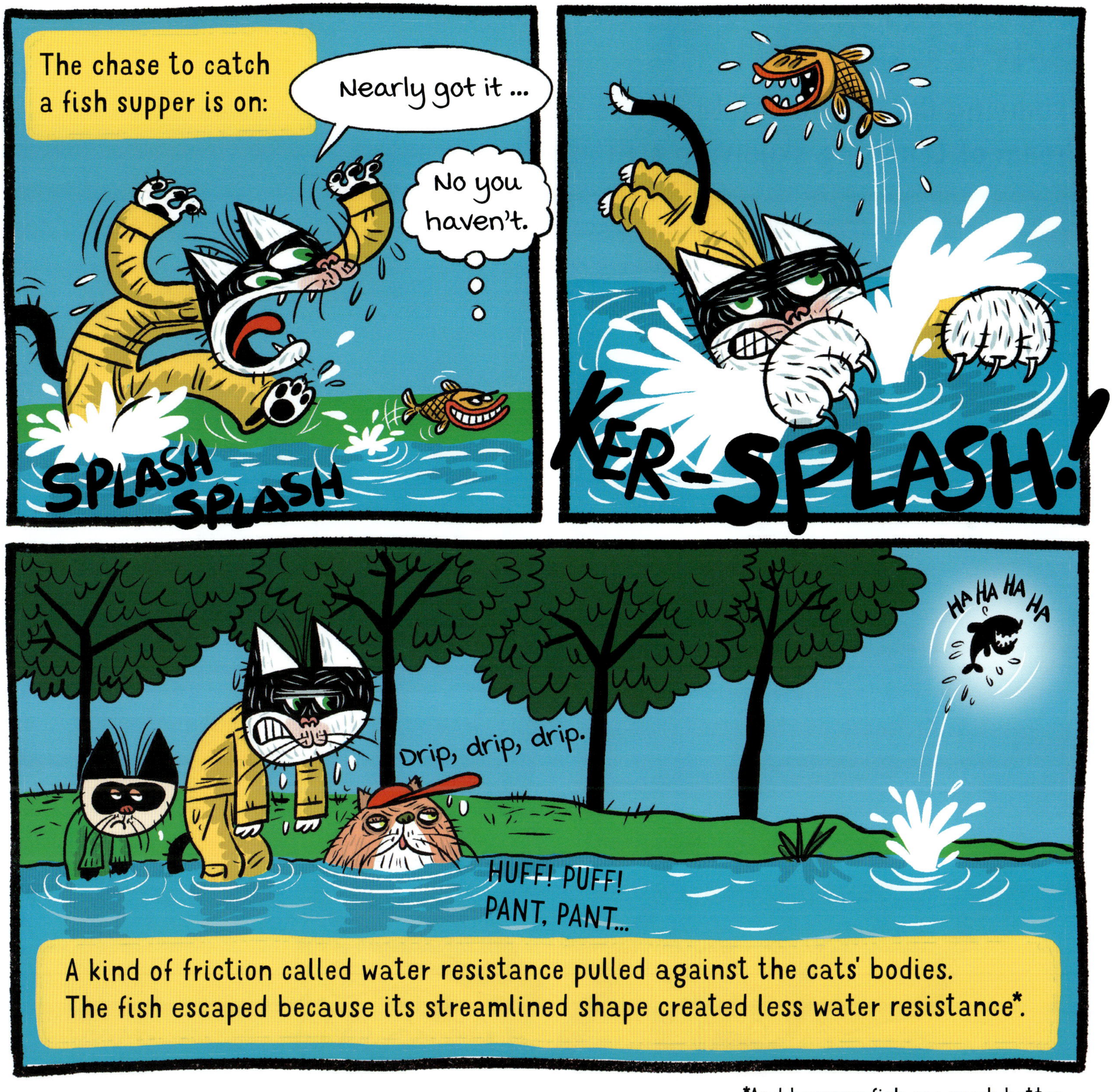

*And because fish are much better at swimming than cats.

# SAFELY ASHORE

Skydiving Cat, you're safely ashore – so is your dream of teaching skydiving still alive?

# BONUS CAT FACTS

1. Cats might not be built for skydiving, but they are good at jumping. Most can jump up to six times their length. If humans could do that, we'd be able to jump nine metres into the air.

2. Cat claws all curve backward. This makes them excellent at climbing up things, but means they have to climb down backward.

3. It's not a good idea to let a cat lick you: their tongues are so rough, they can strip the meat off a bone.

4. Cats like their own place to poo – so indoor cats hate sharing a litter tray.

5. Meowing is something cats only do to communicate with humans.

6. Cats use their tails to communicate. A straight-up tail means 'I'm happy to see you.' A wagging tail means 'You're getting on my nerves.'

7. Cats can't taste sweetness. (They are thought to be the only mammals that can't.)

8. Cat farts smell bad because cats eat a lot of meat. Meat contains a chemical called sulfur. After digestion, this turns into a gas scientists call hydrogen sulfide. Everyone else calls it eggy-fart smell.

# GLOSSARY

**air resistance** – a kind of friction, a pulling force that happens when air and a solid object move past each other

**canopy** – wide, lightweight upper part of a parachute, which catches against the air and slows the parachute's fall

**gas** – material that can change its shape and size to fit its container

**flight** – planned route taken by an aircraft, agreed in advance by the pilot

**fluid** – a material (a liquid or a gas) that can flow and change shape

**friction** – pulling force between two materials that are moving past each other

**level off** – fly at the same height

**liquid** – material that can change its shape to fit a container, but not its size

**magnetism** – force that works on some kinds of metal, which is sometimes a pull, sometimes a push

**mammal** – animal that has some sort of body hair and feeds its young on milk from the mother

**parachute** – device that allows a heavy object to fall through the air more slowly

**skydive** – jump out of an aircraft with a parachute packed up on your back, before opening the parachute and floating to the ground

**solid** – material that is not a fluid, and usually stays the same shape and size

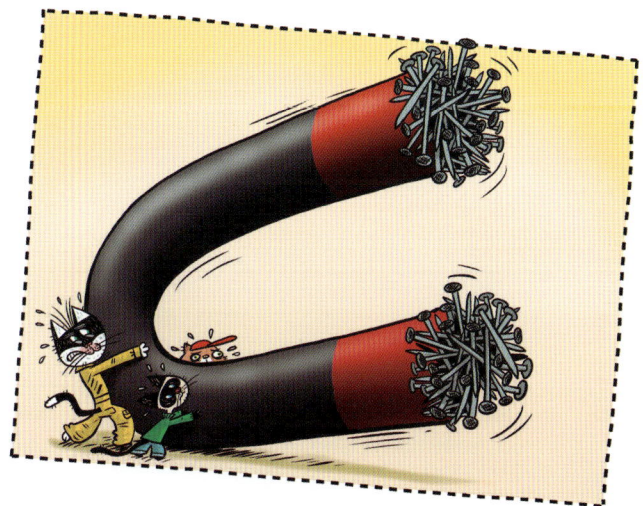

# INDEX

airfield 23
air resistance 10, 11, 31

compass 23

friction 10, 27, 31
fluid 19
flying squirrel 11

gases 19
gravity 6-7, 8, 14, 28

iron 22

lift 18, 19, 29
liquid 19

magnet 22
materials 14-15, 28
matter 14

parachutes 10, 15

streamlined 27

water resistance 27, 29